Being Present

———— ❧ ————

Personal Spaces

m a r i a   k e a n e

PAGE PUBLISHING, INC.
Conneaut Lake, PA

First originally published by Page Publishing 2020

(All sayings added to the Graphics are attributed to Hafiz, the most beloved poet of Persia, (c.1320-1389.)

Cover art and graphic illustrations by maria keane.

ISBN 978-1-64701-858-0 (pbk)
ISBN 978-1-64701-860-3 (hc)
ISBN 978-1-64701-859-7 (digital)

Printed in the United States of America

For my family, who continues to inspire.

If you think I am having more fun
Than anyone else on this plan,
You are absolutely correct.

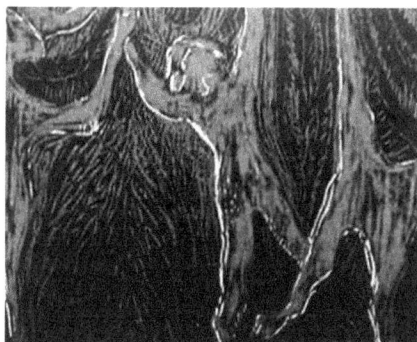

Repair

Nail polish is a liability.
Why did I take time to lacquer them?
This episode is poorly timed.
Cloaked in paint,
I let my hands drown in dishwater.
Can they be cleansed of the secrets beneath?

Fingers paddle pots and pans;
dirt and harsh detergents
erode a mask.
There is no time for repair, but
when the job is done,
I surface and risk exposure.

Shriveled hands cannot hold a pen
or mark ink blurred by damp paper.
I towel tears, blot coolness, and
mold features
to repair grief.

Better to wear soft gloves and
sport a night cream for the chafe
to soothe and heal
with time.

Looking Back...

If this was the first day of my life,
I would not cry at birth, nor
would I mind all those goggling at me.

I would grow up slowly in order to
taste my childhood loves:
skating, swimming, flipping picture cards, and
drawing favorite action figures.

I would fashion my girlishness, flirting
with my eighth-grade favorite guys,
tempting Lotharios in high school,
by rouging my cheeks and
securing a pompadour that made me look taller.

I would dance like a maid from the bowery,
raising my skirt with no crinoline for defense;
my tastes would go beyond sacramental wine.

I would claim eternal inheritance
after remission.
With penitence assured,
I would model the early life of Augustine,
who, like me,
was saved through the prayers of Monica,
the supplication of a faithful mother.

Late Afternoon Tea

There are ways to evade an answer:
a method of restraining talk that turns
conversation into stone.

Wrapped in a world of chatter,
I wait for meaning in a teacup
where leaves remain
clinging to porcelain.

Your soft speech modifies fortune and
alters truth. Outside,
a sunset bathes brambles of truth.
Light paints the dark side of an afternoon.

Confrontation

Did you know me then,
or did you know me when
I was a fragment of a shell
stitched together
between dreaming and daylight?

I am dark now,
a spooked bird
with uncombed hair
squawking with ready beak
to pierce a cloud
for rain.

I face you,
savor sacred promises
though
your eyes intimate failure.

Our lips touch:
communion
honored
only with credit.

Why I Take Good Care of My Brushes

It's important to take a hand in the care of things:
priming paints, wielding clean bristles
to prevent puddles.

Pigments bleed, they gradate:
all wait their turn
to stain the page.

I am a companion in this alchemy
stretching paper with water
where colors trickle down a vertical plane.

Brushes brandish,
resist runaways
to shape pigment on the page.

A thing held in hand,
with plumage,
paints its magic…

Then my talisman,
the wood, wields its dank dance
of invention and design.

Cool Blue Morning

Gases in the atmosphere
give earth
blue light.

I stretch in air,
sinews taut
on wire
between
tall towers.

Like Petit's *Le Coup*,
an ambient gesture:
a pirouette between air and reality.

There is no escape;
I dance.

God
Disguised
As a myriad of things and
Playing a game
Of tag

The Quest

Coffined by silence,
I listen…

You tell me I am God within,
so tell me what I must do.

Your silence stifles intimacy.
My displeasure,
tempered like glass,
inhibits premonition.

I insist upon a response.
Memory woven like medieval tapestry
unravels, a voice
threading my pillow.

The Crucible of Faith

I am astonished by the jokes
God plays.

Voiceless,
in custodial care,
my house rocked to shambles.

I am wrapped in bandages,
wounds hidden from the world.

Then a quiet noise outside;
I am deaf but dare to hope.

I go to church to see if
God is still there.

Lachrymose

The small bucket

on the church bench fills.

The steeple leaks;

tears from angels

weep like candles

melting from the heat of sin:

sorrow for errant mortals.

Saints and Martyrs

Strange
how disaster shapes lives.
Frailty and deaths
may weaken or bolster resolve.

Baptisms of fire immolate ego, and
sacraments
meant only for saints
make new martyrs.

Where is the intervening angel,
the intercessor,
who rescues?

Interment

The hollow from funerals
is already green with grass.

Mounds of flowers smother
weary mourners;
mouths sting from silence.

Each muddy gait
bares wounds
of intimacy.

Rain puddles
a lost faith,
drowns a harsh past.

Memories smile
through grim masks
shielding injury.

Tears salt
the sensitive
from pillars of stone.

Thirst

*(Dark, ancient churches bear boxes that beg
alms for those who wish to view masterpieces,
even for a short time…)*

Children await illumination
for the painting: a woman
carrying an urn.

It hangs dimly, awaiting
adoration from children who,
like coins, huddle in a tempered box.

They await donations from a font
to solace dry throats.
They do not beg for mercy.

They tend the well, labor
in love and light, and stretch hands
wayward to the well.

Their sandals smart on gravel,
crave needs to Jesu for those
with no time to travel.

But I know if you
Pray
Somewhere in this world—
Something good will happen.

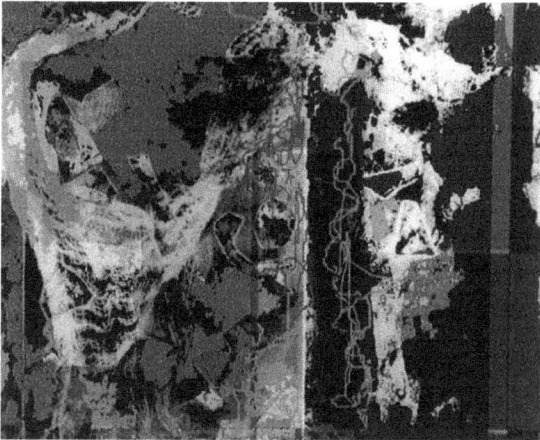

Halcyon Reverie

My head rests
on a pillow of cloud.

I breathe
between thought and reason.
Daylight blinds,
interrupts rest.

I am tempted to roust
thoughts into a poem,
leave the quiet, and
bring it outside.

When I am sure no one is listening,
I recite it in bold tones,
then press it
on a white blanket of paper.

I crumple all,
place it deep in my pocket,
then resurrect it as a failed meditation:
a whisper in a rush of air.

Dissolves in Life

A cloistered scene;
the dreamer drifts
into a haze of nostalgia.

A seamless transition
of linear light stirs animation—
fades in and fades out.

My life of short subjects
emerges: liquid motion
blends and dissolves.

A film blankets vividness,
merges into a frame
of the ephemera, melts reality.

Wavering Steps

Guardians of happiness
murmur about care
of adults who tread aimlessly
in spaces separating
fools from the wise.

Postures of those in need
twist in doubtful directions.
Their feet turn without volition, and
warped speech yields syllables
begging silence.

Their expressions linger with no protest.
Waves of consciousness
overrun clarity, contradict
restraints of behavior
with unique mishaps.

Is there prophecy from
the fruits of heaven where
everything awkward moves with joy,
though hands clap and feet
trip over ridges in the earth?

These disabled stand with philosophers,
with outstretched hands and fragile strength.
They parade reluctantly, ageless children,
stalking with padded feet
through gardens of spiked fern.

Wavering Steps

Their caretakers
share loyal affection
as protectors; they choose
to aid powerless clients
with feeble ambition.

These guardians of happiness complain,
though they continue to care for those who
tread aimlessly. Custodians tolerate love:
a reproach failing indulgence
from a diffident, blissful world.

Now, Forever

My body canvas
paints emotion:
a palette of
the God within.

My mortal years
crystallize hope,
melt doubt into
shades of immortality.

Visions

I wake with fright forecasting images complete,
subconscious scenes, previsions of coincidence.

My resting bones and fleeting soul must meet
prophetic glimpses tried by will and chance.

These schizoid paths of fitful visualizations
become clairvoyant gilding circumstance.

They cast my rusted footsteps into fortunes:
a transport dreaming to a cosmic dance.

Free will can tear my ragged world to tatters;
my mirror clouds and fails to rape reality.

These filtered dreams may only serve to shatter;
failed hopes reduce my soul to frailty.

My waltz, a dance with earthly ordinary beings,
persists to shape my manufactured dreams.

Renewal

Rooted like a gnarled tree,
I bend and drop heavy branches
on hard ground.

Uncertain rhythms clock time,
beat idle space
between slow steps.
My feet slap firmly on stone
like palms
whipping the Lenten season.

Redbirds fly through branches
trusting seasons
with better faith than I.
Forsythia burst
through an untimely spring:
blossoms strain to dance.

Deep into my garden, I dig
to force the season and
let dirt fly,
clearing a path
toward immortality.

A lover's pain is like holding one's breath
Too long
In the middle of a vital performance.

Moon Phase

Your personality
prefers to hide
your far side.

There are secrets
you harbor
like the moon,
whose orbit deceives.

I prefer to indulge
with musings of you:
constellations
within your orbital sphere.

Moss cradles us
from the night air, and
heaven mirrors us
in a languid pool.

The full moon,
though bathed
in sunlight,
blankets us in shadow.

Ethereal You

I cannot remember your inviting lips,
not to be forgotten.

I cannot hold what slips far away,
not without an echo.

Memories persist,
not to bury the past.

A shadow veils the sweetness
of your wild taste.

Coffee at the Nighthawk Café

We drink darkness
in limbo.

The two of us
with cold at our backs.
This late hour
assures no intimacy.

Silence, the only sound unspoken,
black and bitter as the coffee,
fills space and time:
dissolves like sugar.

Waning Youth

A cobweb of moon
flares and falters,
reflecting a virgin mirror.

I scour the identity of a mask
repulsed by light.
I thought by now it would stop,

but it still happens—
an unrelenting ache
when we lock hands.

Why do I gaze at your face
to find your raison d'être:
a beauty that embellished your
energy and grace
once there?

Dawn

It is no wonder
that the moon
peeks relentlessly before
it gives up our night.

A brief evening
graces affection
to blanket
our warm bodies.

Is this too short
an *aubade*
for secrets we share?

The Tryst

The pearl of Venus dissolves in
the crescent moon's chalice.

I scoop the stars
to brandish the order of heaven.

I glean celestial light
while stumbling through the dark.
This could be the last summer we know.

I am naked to the fire of your beauty.
Our breath bathes us in the night air,
cooling the ashes of passion.

It is a naive man who thinks we are not
Engaged in a fierce battle.

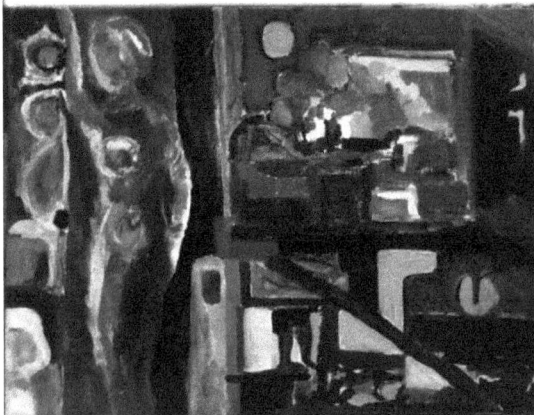

Moving Along

Someone waves and beckons
for seed to crust the earth.
A jeweled wheel keeps time alive,
inviolate, tempting infinity.

Life condenses moments through mist:
a compromise of liquid memory.
Wings crackle as night spills
rime on a black counter.

I claw my fingers through dust and frost
to test survival.
My will fluctuates on a hinge of choice.
My star drops fast to what I will become.

Confessional

Damask veils
the face that money makes,
sequestered in a boarded space.

The face that money makes,
silken as water,
cleanses gelatinous crime.

The face that money makes
gnaws smiles,
before moments of
retaliation or prayer.

(Daisy Bates is best known for her involvement in the struggle to integrate Central High School in Little Rock, Arkansas (1957). As an adviser to nine black students trying to attend a previously all-white school, she was a pivotal figure in that seminal moment of the civil rights movement.)

For Daisy Bates

Daisy, you rode the wheels of Rosa's bus,
paved the walk
when the Feds *punched* your ticket.

They failed
to guide
nine "long black shadows"

to pass the segregates
who built everything on fear.
I wanted to be there holding hands with you,

holding on—
feeling the heat of hate,
tripping the troops.

For Daisy Bates

But I remember
shuffling my past:
a student

shredding thoughts
to dream paper dreams.
I did not know

the cost of
the price of a ticket,
anywhere,

except
on a Madison Avenue bus.

Beyond the Light

Why do you tempt a manic moon
to spin and swivel, or
is this your witness to brute beasts
where bluebirds bob and
starlings sing?

Within the lies of deception,
your gauzy pretense
twirls a parasol,
dances in a
cloister of glass.

There is no way to hide your anger
in a cloak of froth.

Your fist demolishes
a fragile palace:
shards illuminate spirit lamps.

Our landscape
tangles fears with deceit
in the prowl of night.

I Remember…

I remember we forced our baby's weak steps
to walk.
I remember she fell on concrete,
skinning her swollen knee.
I remember
stopping by her silent swing.
I remember lifting hard
to saddle her in comfort.
I remember someone steel-bound in a chair
crying with resistance.

Desiderata

I wish for a robe of water to cleanse
the naked. Those, who, stricken with
guilt, reveal appetites of the flesh.
They think they relinquish their eternity and
stagger with guilt toward salvation,
denying their humanity without embracing
the blessed fruits of mortality.

Love is the funeral pyre
Where the heart must lay its body.

Betrayal

A palette of stone
crushes lavender,
releases incense,
revives memories.

Disgrace bathes in grasses,
prickles the spine.

Active hearts suffer,
maintain innocence.
Stigmata persist,
resist healing.

Stones sear flesh,
purge offense,
despite the cost
of not loving enough.

For You

I thought it might not last that long;
 our love was always measured
 to hear the music of your song.

I want to think of that first song
you gave to me when all was treasure.
I thought it might not last that long.

We thought our love was really strong,
 the way I sauntered in our leisure
 to hear the music of your song.

I did not think that we were wrong.
 Though it may not last forever,
I thought it still might last that long.

Did we inflate our liaison?
Still I'll always be the proud possessor
 to hear the music of your song.

Your Judas Kiss

Lies are flames licking death;
they are nothing until they arrive.

There is no return
from your past.

Your rocky path,
too hard.
So here you are,
splintered wood—
swinging from a tree.

Confrontation Realized

Truth allows me to
shake your shoulders,
beg answers
until I am weak.

You stand tall,
brittle as the moment
when
every question begs an answer.

My harsh inquiries
persist
discharged with effort
as if pulling a crank.

Our mutual waste
runs through us,
cleansing rivulets,
making us chaste.

You relent,
knowing that our vows,
elastic, stretched to their limit,
may not be reinvented.

Losing a Child in Water

The Natural Bridge yawns wide,
spews De De and Pa Pa
past the gorge onto
white crystal sands of
Virginia Beach.

Strain your moorings,
mournful father.
Have her climb your mountain back.

Let her curl those clinging feet round
your soft midsection until
it claws the flesh you nurtured.

Imaginary beings float in sandcastles,
swirl over the child
abandoned to the sea.

She thrashes through biting sand,
a deep funeral force
writhing from tentacles of seaweed.

They suck sand,
spew foam;
she chokes with brine.

Imaginary beings float,
swirl over the child,
disjoining the child from the man.

In Memoriam

Absence is a hard task.

I need to find a new way of walking
without shedding skin.
I swerve toward a picture frame
draped dark with purple.

You must know who I am and
why I light a candle for my friend.

I look for something not deserved:
the applause of a waterfall,
a jewel pried loose from a mortal crown.

I walk into the storm;
sheets of rain break
like glass:
infinity hums.

I whisper a solemn vow before
my next breath.
I dare to touch the hand
that knocks at paradise.

Words from you have reached Him
And tilled a golden field inside.

Night Swim

Water bathes me; I shimmer,
glisten,
rippling in the night.

I paddle, float
in my liquid bed.
A soft caress molds me,
warms me,
in the wash of summer.

I submerge in darkness,
seek a baptism
bathing me clean.

I emerge in light,
break silence with
a splash,
propelled with joy.

The Wonder

Whispered prayer sanctifies space
for eternal banquets.
While others taste bread,
famine remains my feast.
This dearth of consecration
spills wine:
stains not to be hidden.

Garden Space

A putti fountain
sprays water; I
bless myself
remembering the purity
of baptism.

Past vows broken—
then renewed;
ambivalent faith
sways to the rhythm
of a garden hammock.

Splintered wood of
a firethorn
boasts red bloodberries,
mortifies flesh, and inebriates
with sacramental wine.

I crush the slender, slate-blue
leaves of fallen lavender,
recalling the musk of
the bishop's oil, marking foreheads
of the *confirmandi.*

I ascend.
My cape of garden colors
flaps loosely
in a prevailing wind.
I am buoyant.

On Sea and Shore...

In the middle of June,
weather was perfect for high tides,
when full moons tempt
female spider crabs to emerge.
Their blood, light blue,
is colored by a copper base.
Pulled up to the high-tide line,
they spawn, dig, deposit
pearly green bird-shot-sized eggs,
fertilize, then abandoned,
the waves washed sand
over their nests.

Beyond the moon,
morning light and dunes
invite a solitary walk
where whirling winds
smart the shore and
burn the cheek with sand.
Similar currents sway sails
into the bay, cutting like scissors,
breaking free the anchor chains of self.

On the shore,
butterflies flutter;
Queen Anne's lace attracts bees.
Breezes chart a path of monotony
for vacationers, while persistent hard-shells
abandon the beach,
resolute to survive
the ocean's resonance.

The Respite

We sit beneath the canopy of
a persimmon tree.
It drops bitter berries
on the hard ground.

The heat of the afternoon
cooks conversation
as we pull words
from dry mouths.

Swallows like ribbons
stripe sunlight
below a smudged sky.
Being present

in this quiet green
transforms us.
We look heavenward
through bare branches,

spiking Constable skies
where red sunsets
blush to a fading orange
of spent seeds.

The Child Who...

I am at the velvet edge of exploration.
I listen to beats beneath the earth
separating groves of blood roses.

I am the child who smells earth after rain,
who watches trails of ants that go nowhere,
who plucks the air just after

the monarch leaves its milkweed,
who kneels in moist wells
of fern below
a ceiling of leaves

beneath a bruising sky,
tangled in a thin layer of dust.
I watch the falcon glide
above the mottled hologram of earth.

I dig small hollows
in the shadow of the oak
to cover the limp
green garden snake.

My garden dance
becomes redundant.
I look beyond a patch of grass
with stringy roots—
uncertainties that beg

The Child Who...

the sun to wink
between the clouds.
I shrug off origami cranes
attempting flight for those
thin promises of tomorrow.

Previously published poems by the Author:

Thirst in Being There, Page Publishing Inc. 2018
In Memoriam in Being There, Page Publishing Inc. 2018
The Child Who…, northofoxford word press 2017

Maria Keane: Poet and Printmaker

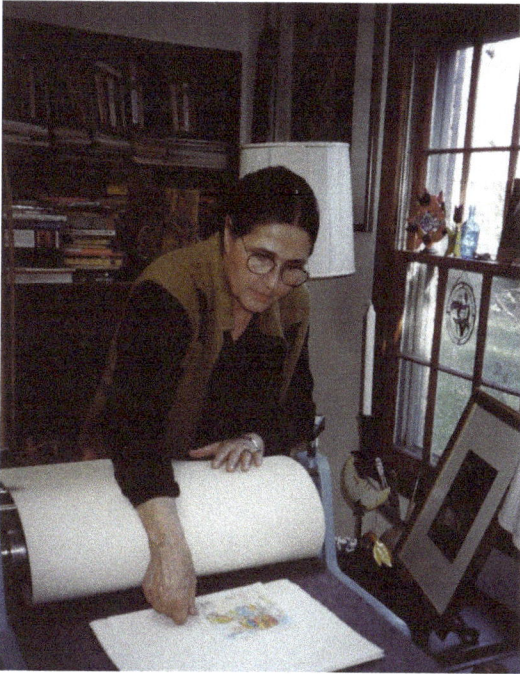

About the Author

Maria Keane is an award-winning poet and visual artist. She offers in this collection an invitation to embrace a life of creativity: the catalyst for savoring quiet moments of contentment. Personal experiences with family and friends enrich awareness and encourage a spirit of gratitude necessary to accept life's challenges.

Her former volume of poetry, *Being There*, was awarded a First in Creative Writing by the National League of America Press Women in 2019. Her visual art received a Professional Fellowship in Works on Paper and was jointly awarded from the NEA and the Delaware Division of the Arts in 1997.

CPSIA information can be obtained
at www.ICGtesting.com
Printed in the USA
BVHW061828060421
604345BV00009B/920

9 781647 018580